Your Secret Present *for* Christmas

Let Your Wishes Come True

Kateryna Markhanova

Contents

A Personal Preface

This book is dedicated to help you make your wishes, dreams, intentions, or desires (however you would like to call them) come true! We will work with your conscious and subconscious mind to ease your way of achieving and receiving what you want. I will use for this purpose my personal successful experience of manifestation and knowledge that I have gained from the last 12 years of studies of success principles, human psychology, numerology, and some universal laws, as well as alignment with universal energy flows. The Universe has immense energy; if we are able to align with it, our wishes, dreams and goals will manifest with ease. Often, people are blocking their own way into getting what they want without even recognizing it. Many obstacles are hidden in the subconscious mind, which is why hypnotherapy can be so effective in addressing issues and resolving problems, as it works with the various layers of the subconscious mind. I experienced that a lot with RTT hypnotherapy, both with myself and my many clients. My tasks here are to guide you in the manifestation journey, help you release mental barriers, enhance your resourceful emotional states, and connect with your subconscious mind so that your wishes come true.

Additionally, I intend to help you connect to yourself, to your environment, and the Universal energy. In this approach, I am considering the pillars of manifestation as time, space, matter, and energy, with you as the centre of all of it. It is said that the Magic started with an internal state. Therefore, I strongly recommend that you follow the exercises closely and allow yourself to feel and enjoy the process. I developed meditations to accompany you in this process. It is advisable to do these meditations as well. Please visit my website https://imlifejoysuccess.com/ for more information.

Please carefully read the Q&A section to understand the ecology of the wishes. It is important to adhere to it to avoid any negative karmic consequences for yourself and the people close to you. Please follow the methodology step by step and do all exercises as they are described. There are some alternative exercises for you to choose from on certain days. Every day and every step within this process has a special meaning and will lead you to make your wishes come true. I cannot guarantee it will absolutely work for you, as there are so many layers of materialization and manifestation principles, but this process will greatly increase your chances. It is definitely worth doing it!

Let your Christmas presents make your life merrier. Share your success stories with me via the website https://imlifejoysuccess.com/. I will be happy to read them and share them with your permission. Let us together inspire more people in the world!

Merry Christmas!

With Love,
Kateryna Markhanova

This book belongs to

Name _______________________________

Surname _______________________________

____

____

____

____and____

____

First Steps

First of all, please sign this book with your name (full name as it appears on your official documents, so it is clear for whom the presents' delivery shall be). Please do not use nicknames or shortened names, as your full name gives you the most strength and energy. I will not go into details about why this is so important, because it would be another therapeutic topic to discuss. If you are in denial of your full name as it appears on your official documents, you can write in brackets the name you like to be called. For instance, Thomas Gerald Smith (Tom Smith).

Then, write in each line with gratitude to the Universe, yourself, and the Christmas Spirit.

Then, you can start with the instructions for the first day, the 17th of December, following the exercises for each day until the final day, the 25th of December. Do not skip a day, and do not complete exercises for two days in one day, etc.

Once you have defined your main wish for the Christmas present, you will need to write it on a paper and put it in an envelope. You can also find an envelope in a color you love; it is also possible, but not necessary, to choose a color based on the essence of your wish. Here I would apply the wisdom of chakras. Let me give you some examples:

A wish for a healthy baby to be born, to have strong health, to have more life energy, a new residence (red), a wish related to having more pleasure (orange), wish related to social status, for example, to get married, get a new car, a nice watch, a branded bag (yellow), a wish to get more love, true love, create a charity organisation (green), a wish related to becoming a speaker, gain more visibility in society (light blue), wish related to gaining clarity on strategies for a company, seeing beneficial opportunities for some projects or just in life (dark blue), a wish related to understanding your mission, to being aligned with your mission, to being aligned to the higher power (violet).

I would recommend you read the Q&A section before you start, but this is not necessary. If during this journey you would have a question, you might find your answer in the Q&A section. Otherwise, please DM me on Instagram. I will be picking some questions and answering them in my stories or reels.

Let's get it started!

Christmas Journey

Welcome to Day 1. Today is the 17th of December.

Start this day with envisioning and asking yourself:

- What do I really want?
- What do I like?
- How do I want my future to be like?
- What can I do for myself today?
- What am I thankful for today?
- What would bring me joy and satisfaction?
- Who am I today? Who would I like to become?
- What does my dream life look like?"

Start to answer these questions on a sheet of paper. As you go along the day, write the thoughts that are coming to you related to these questions. Maybe you notice that you are thinking that this "dream-future" is not possible, this is all right—write that down too. These thoughts could highlight some of your negative beliefs and blocks. However, the main focus of this day should be on the main questions above.

Everything that is possible for you to do today, please do it. If you do not have time, choose three to four simple things that you can do according to the question, "What can I do for myself today?"

For instance:

o "Drink fresh-pressed orange juice"—just go for it!

o "Watch a movie"—watch it today!

o "Have a coffee or tea in a nice place downtown"— just go for it!

o "Meet a friend somewhere spontaneously"—if your friend is up to it too!

o "Start to read a new book"—please start, even if it would be a half of a page for this day.

o "Tell your close people compliments or words of love"—just say it!

o "Take a warm bath", etc.

I would recommend you avoid anything fully unhealthy for your body; the body should be the first alliance to get what you want in life. Therefore, it is the individual responsibility of each of us to treat our bodies well. Additionally, I would recommend you avoid, as much as possible, communication with people who can put doubts on what you are doing or complain a lot about their own problems. It consumes a lot of your personal energy without you noticing it, and on top of that, such interaction can plant negative inceptions in your mindset or reinforce your limiting beliefs. This is definitely not serving you.

Some tips on how to deal with "negativity":

o Try to change the focus of this person to something else.

o Reduce the time of communication with this person.

o   Overtake the lead in the conversation and change the subject to something positive.

o   Make compliments about the person's clothes, hair, makeup, and the like.

o   Thank a person for anything good that he/she did for you in the past.

All this will help you win the time and protect your energy and positive aspirations for your future.

Ideally, you would pick two to three things to do today in which you do not have to depend on anyone else, because if your friend is busy or that particular place you would like to go to is closed, it would create disappointment. This does not serve you for the first day. On the other hand, it is a good day to spend in the good company of close friends and enjoy the time together.

Each time you do something from your wish list, tell yourself, "I can do it.".

At the end of the day, ask yourself:

•   If I could have all the necessary resources to feel comfortable and sure about the future, what would I do?

Write it down.

Before going to sleep, look at the answers you wrote during the day. Put those notes aside, close your eyes and think about what is your one wish that you would like to come true. What is the dream that you want the Christmas Spirit to help you realize in life? What is the secret Christmas present that you wish to receive? Imagine you have it now—what do you feel? If you feel lots of tension in your body, it might indicate that this wish is not yours or "too big" for you (refer to Q&A section). Can you think about anything else? Imagine that you got it—how do you feel? If you are getting feelings of happiness, joy, and love, these are good markers for this wish.

If there is any wish you would like to have with your partner (wife/ husband), you can talk about it and describe it to each other by sharing your thoughts and feelings about it. If this is something you want but are not sure if your partner wants it, you can keep it to yourself as your secret, but once you are visualizing it, do not include any faces of the people close to you to mind the wish-ecology (refer to Q&A section).

(The Day 1 Meditation "Being myself" is advisable.)

Day 2. Today is the 18th of December.

On the second day, you need to make a space for your wish to come true.

Task 1:

Please look around the place you live in and search for things that represent the barriers to your wish. The first thoughts that come into your mind are true. You need to gather all these things, look at each of them saying, "Thank you, but you do not serve me anymore. It is time to say goodbye". During this day, you need to get rid of all these things. Please decide how you will do this: For instance, place them in the trash, bring them to a second-hand shop, or recycle containers, or if it is possible, put them on a street side in your neighbour- hood for anyone to take away for free (if this is allowed in your community). Please do it with good intentions; if some- thing is perceived as a barrier for you, this may not be the case for someone else. You can leave the things with the thought, "May you be found by a new owner for the good of all". The intention and the words you use are highly important. Keep them positive.

If you come up with the thought that "all the things sur- rounding me are the barriers", this can be a sign of self-sabo- tage or a message for you that your wish is not something that you genuinely want, but rather family or social-driven expec- tations. This is a good day to revisit your wish and recon- sider it. If you have the thought "my old car, or this flat, or house is a barrier for me," and obviously you can't give up on them within such a short time, maybe you would like to set a goal to move to a new flat or buy another car. In this way, you are helping yourself to manifest what you want in life. Additionally, find the little things that you perceive as barriers to your wish.

It is very important to free your living space from these barriers until the 24th of December. Please remain consistent with your decision until this task completed; it is not helpful if you change your mind the next day, or in some hours, regarding what you will say "goodbye" to.

Additionally, I recommend you read Marie Kondo's book "Magic Cleaning". However, it is optional, and you can do it next year if you like.

Task 2:

During this day, please find an opportunity to walk with bare feet on the ground or grass to feel the Earth. If it is too cold outside to do so, depending on where you live, you can simply go for a walk or a run in nature. In the evening, look at the stars and moon and think about what you are thankful for in your life.

(The Day 2 Meditation "Making the space" is advisable.)

Day 3. Today is the 19th of December.

This day should be spent in joyful and bright ways with friends, family members, etc. Spend this day in ease and take it as it goes. During this day, you need to have on you, or with you, something that symbolizes status—it can be anything. If you have some beautiful jewels, put them on and dress up. You need to feel within yourself as festive, joyful and content as possible. If it is possible for you to look at the sun and think about everything good that you have in your life, do so!

Here are some things that you could do this day, but are not limited to:

- Watching a funny comedy show.
- Having dinner in an especially nice restaurant.
- Having a party.
- Going to a concert or stand-up comedy.
- Going for a beautiful date. (By the way, you can have a date with your partner even if you are living together, married and have kids.)
- Having dinner at home, but do special decorations (for instance, put up candles, flowers, napkins, etc.)

Enjoy this day, and before you go to sleep, inwardly tell yourself thanks for this day and everything you have, and you will have much more in your life. Feel it.

(The Day 3 Meditation "Sun" is advisable.)

Day 4. Today is the 20ᵗʰ of December.

On this day, it is important to recognize and feel your family connections, your family, and where you come from, and to give this attention. Perhaps you can connect with your family members (if you know that such communication will bring you joy), or maybe you want to remind them about the upcoming Christmas celebration. If not, it might be better to simply think about your family members, perhaps remembering someone who is no longer with you, and to express gratitude for the good things they did for you. There is always something good that people in our families have done for us. If possible, let them know this over the phone, via text or out loud. It is important to feel your state of gratitude and to be present in it.

(The Day 4 Meditation "Family" is advisable.)

If you are a business owner, it is a good day for you to envision the additional direction of your business, maybe an additional source of revenue streams the next year. Let your ideas be known to your partners or business assistant, and have a little kickoff and plant a seed that might flourish soon.

If you are a couple who would like to have a child, you can discuss how you both will be playing with your child, where you will be buying clothing for your child, how you will be teaching your child to walk, talk, etc.

Additionally, on this day, you can visit some art exhibitions or look at any art collections at your home (this can be anything; some paintings created by your children are art too), or you can watch a good family movie together or play a family game at home.

Day 5. Today is the 21st of December.

The winter solstice usually falls on December 21st or 22nd in the Northern Hemisphere. On this day, we experience the shortest day and the longest night of the year. The exact date may vary slightly from year to year, but you can generally count on it being around the 21st or 22nd of December. This is a special time because after the winter solstice, the days start to get longer, and the sun becomes more present on Earth.

It is important to spend this day in harmony with the environment, think about the elements we share: Water, Air-Wind, Earth, Fire. Think about the enormous potential of this planet sustaining us, providing us water and plants and animals. Think about how we are part of this planet, too. Feel all these natural resources that we are a part of and reflect on your gratitude for this world and all it provides us.

(The Day 5 Meditation "Earth" is advisable.)

On this day, you can give spontaneous presents to children you know; it can be your own children (if you have them), or children you know well.

Also, on this day, take the time to think about the teachers who are supporting you in your learning process. Do you have any favourite teachers? Why are they your favourite? Take some time to think with appreciation of the teachers who help you learn more about this world.

Day 6. Today is the 22nd of December.

During this day, think of all the things that you managed to do well and all of the spontaneous or desired presents you got in your life. Take a sheet of paper and write all these down. You need to come up with 71 points. It is important that this is something you enjoyed and that it was easy for you. Additionally, think if you had appreciation from others for what you did—write it, too.

Examples: It can be something very easy, such as, "My friend brought a sandwich to school and she shared it with me". "I finished reading the book _______". "I easily passed the _____________ exam", etc.

Once you have got these 71 points, please give yourself appreciation for all these experiences in your past. More to come! Feel the gratitude in you and all around you.

Then, you will need to define three wishes for Christmas and write them down:

1st **wish** – Something that you know will definitely come true in the near future. It can be something like in January, spend the weekend _________, buy a new coffee machine, etc.

2nd **wish** – Something "nice to have"—this can be whatever you want, but if it does not happen, it is not a big deal. As a second wish, you can take "too big" (refer to Q&A section).

3rd **wish** – your main wish "Your Secret Present for Christmas", something you want dearly to come true and will bring you many resourceful emotional states, such as joy, love, gratitude, interest, passion and drive to life.

Technique "My wish came true":

Please use the present tense for all three wishes and something that is happening now on three separate papers.

Imagine that your 3rd **wish** came true. Please answer the questions below on a separate A4 paper. If you need several papers, that is fine, too. Use your imagination!

1. How do you feel? Describe these feelings.
2. What becomes possible when your dream came true? Write that down.
3. What do you think when your wish came true? Write that down.
4. With whom will you share that your dream came true?
5. Describe your life after you got this present: what do you see, what do you smell, what do you touch, what do you do?
6. Does this wish have any positive impact on other people? Describe that, too.
7. Who are you when your wish came true? (For more insights, refer to the Identity section.)

You can spray some perfume on all these papers. Write your name on each of them and put all these papers in the envelope that you purchased (refer to the section First Steps). Close the envelope. On this Christmas envelope, write your name and the following:

- With gratitude and acceptance, this or something better in divine appropriate timing for the Highest Good.

Place this envelope under the Christmas tree (if you have one) or at any other place where you have prepared Christmas festive presents for yourself and your loved ones.

(The Day 6 Meditation "My dream came true" is advisable.)

The next day, go to any shop and buy yourself anything that can represent that your wish came true.

Day 7. Today is the 23rd of December.

On this day, you can go to a beautiful place that you enjoy (a café, a restaurant, an art gallery, a cinema, etc.); it would be great if you could go there by the most comfortable mode of transportation possible.

If you need to stay at home, think about in what circumstance you had some victory, maybe you won a price or you won in a game; this should be something inspiring to reflect on.

Alternately, you can watch some documentary movies about famous athletes, artists or actors.

(The Day 7 Meditation "Gratitude" is advisable.)

Just enjoy this day!

Day 8. Today is the 24ᵗʰ of December.

This day is all about you preparing for the Christmas evening—relaxing, celebrating and enjoying.

Before you go to sleep, hold your Christmas envelope; think of all the merry and blessed times in your life.

Before falling asleep, imagine the Christmas Spirit coming to you and giving you lots of presents that make you happy and fulfilled.

Day 9. Today is the 25th of December.

This day is all about the Christmas celebration and having some time off. If you must work on this day, feel the Christmas vibes anyway, as they are all around you today!

This day, just do what you planned to do. Think of all the good things and opportunities that life has to offer, think of all your beloved people, and plan a more joyful time!

On this day, place your Christmas envelope between the days 22nd and 23rd of December. Then put your book with this envelope to your personal belongings, for instance, on a shelf or into a wardrobe.

Live your life in lovely anticipation.

Identity

Perhaps you have heard of Identity, but allow me now to guide you through the concept of Identity in "Neurological Levels."

The concept of "Neurological Levels" in Neuro-Linguistic Programming (NLP) was introduced by Robert Dilts. This model offers a framework for understanding human experience and behaviour across various levels, including environment, behaviour, capabilities, beliefs and values, identity and spirituality. Dilts' contributions have significantly shaped the fields of NLP, coaching and personal development, making his work essential for anyone looking to deepen their understanding of transformation and growth.

This concept helps to align your goal, intention, wish and desire to achieve with an identity perspective. This could enable you to integrate this identity into yourself, your mindset.

You can do this technique at any point of time when you have time for it. I worked with it many times and modified it a bit by enhancing it based on my experience and learnings. There are also other available versions. However, this one includes important elements such as states (emotional states) and body integration.

What you need to do:

Please take eight pieces of paper; they should be big enough to write one to two words on them, and once you put them on the floor, you should be able to clearly read them and be able stand on each of them.

Paper 1: Environment
Paper 2: Behaviour
Paper 3: Capabilities / Skills
Paper 4: States
Paper 5: Thoughts / Beliefs
Paper 6: Values
Paper 7: Identity
Paper 8: Mission

Then, put these papers on the floor in one line so that you can move from one paper to the other one making a step ahead. It is important to do in this way because your body helps you to change the anchor so that your mind helps you to catch and identify what is needed here on each level.

To start, move from Paper 1 to Paper 8, and then back from Paper 8 to Paper 1. On each level, ask yourself the questions that are listed below and write them down. Once you reach Paper 8, while going back, ask yourself the same questions and see or feel if there is anything else you can note.

Here we go (please be precise while answering these questions):

1. **Environment:** Where am I? With whom am I? What do I see around me? What else do I see around me? What else could I see around me? What do I smell? What do I touch?

2. **Behaviour:** What do I do? How do I behave? What action do I take? What are my routines? What is my body language?

3. **Capabilities/ Skills:** What can I do? What are my skills? How do I react? How do I adapt my behaviour?
4. **States:** What are my emotional states? How do I feel? How does my body feel?
5. **Thoughts/ Beliefs:** What am I thinking about? What else am I thinking about? What are my daily thoughts? In what do I believe? What are my beliefs?
6. **Values:** What are my values? What are my priority values?
7. **Identity:** Who am I?
8. **Mission:** What is my mission?

After you complete this task, thank yourself. If you want, you can write a story about it, record it for yourself and listen to it from time to time. You will feel when you no longer need to listen to this recording. It would mean this story is integrated into you. However, I would recommend working through this story with a skilled, experienced coach, because unintentionally, you could install limiting beliefs into your mindset. Therefore, if you are unsure, just do this technique once; it will be enough and very beneficial for you!

How "big" could my wish/dream/present be?

Your wish can be as big as you wish it to be. If you feel doubtful and have not had great experiences of your wishes coming true, you could make this wish as "nice to have" and your main wish chose something more "realistic" for you for the first time. Once it is fulfilled, go BIG.

How do I know if my wish is too "big" for me?

There is a certain understanding that in order to manifest the desires, a person must have enough personal energy and personal scale. This can be trained and evolved through different techniques to get on the level so that you can own your wishes or desires and manifest them easily. If it is not the case, you feel like, "It is never going to happen", or once you do, the technique "My wish came true" (22nd Day December), you feel a pressure / heaviness in your body, or sort of fear, guilt, or panic. This could mean that "the wish is too big to handle", so you are not ready for it, or this is not your true wish. Maybe you want something only because your friend has it, or because this is something your mother or father wanted you to do, etc. There are also ways to do a diagnostic check of your situation so that you can gain clarity and increase your energy/personal scale. Make this wish as "nice to have" and choose something else to be your main wish or Christmas present.

Why do I have to do these tasks when they don't seem to be connected and do not make logical sense? Can I skip some of them?

The famous quote of Albert Einstein says, "Insanity is doing the same thing over and over again and expecting different results." Therefore, this is something that we are looking for, in particular, something different and not logical. I would highly recommend you do all the tasks (if it is possible for you).

How can I cultivate the feeling of gratitude?

You need to think about it as habit. In order to create a habit, you need to repeat it many times. Some individuals need 21 days, some two months, some half a year. Take a paper and write all the people to whom you are grateful.

Then, I would recommend you start thinking about the person to whom you are the most grateful. Start to remember all the good things this person did for you and feel this gratitude. You can start to describe this feeling of gratitude. Maybe you feel the warmth inside your body, you hear some thoughts and you perceive it as a certain vibration or light. Then you can spread out this feeling all around you and enjoy it for a moment. Afterwards, you can gather it inside yourself in your thoughts. The next day, repeat it. You can do it as many days as you want. At some point in time, you will definitely know that you feel the gratitude.

Can I do this not during Christmas time but any time later during the year?

This methodology is created exactly for these days in December as I considered Universal law here, Sun energy awakening, meaning of numbers, etc.

Can I wish to marry my boyfriend ("name of the boyfriend")?

You can do so, if you and your boyfriend have discussed it and you make the plans for the wedding. The wish would be more concerning when it is the "perfect wedding" for you.

If you are not engaged, and you and your boyfriend did not discuss and align on it, I would not recommend doing so. Maybe this is not the person you are meant to live happily with. I am convinced that such decisions and wishes concerning bigger steps in life should not be focused on a particular person.

Therefore, I recommend that your marriage-related wish start with, "I am happily married to a loyal, *adjective, adjective, adjective* man. We live together in our comfortable home. We are enjoying doing _________________________ (fill the blank) together. I feel loved, amazing, blissful, and grateful for my partner."

Can I wish to get pregnant?

This is not a complete wish. You will need to formulate the wish, as in "get pregnant and give birth to a healthy child, with whom I (I and my partner) will have lots of joy in life."

Can I wish to move to another country?

Yes, you can. Please always be specific and indicate your move having positive circumstances. If you have a family, you would need to consider the "buy in" of other family members. Unconsciously, we know who would be against our wish to come true. If these people are significant for you, this could sabotage your own wish to come true.

Can my partner and I wish the same?

Yes, you can. In fact, if you are a couple, you can reinforce the wish to come true if you are aligned on it in a harmonious way.

Can I set a specific time for my wish?

You can unless you feel it puts pressure on you. In spiritual practises, it is said to indicate "in divine appropriate timing". I recommend focusing on your feelings and the emotional state you want to experience once your wish is realized, rather than on a specific time. You could indicate, for instance, "If possible, next year". In this way, there is no "real" pressure. The less pressure you put on your wish, the better.

Can I wish for good health for my child?

If you are the mother or father of a child who is not well, it is best to pray for their health and bless them to live a good life. A mother's prayer holds strong power!

For Christmas, choose a wish that brings you happiness and joy.

If I have Ebook, how shall I proceed?

If you bought an Ebook or received it as a gift, please take an A4 paper and handwrite all the information on the page "this book belongs to". Keep this page with the envelope containing your wishes. Place everything in one of your favorite spots or among your personal belongings at home.

Afterword

Congratulations on the completion of "Your Secret Present for Christmas". Well done!

Now, I recommend you not be too attached to the outcome. Meaning if there is something you could do, take the necessary actions.

Please avoid self-criticism and encourage yourself on your way to get what you want. Stay positive and appreciate yourself.

I know it is easy to say that and doing it can be very hard, but believe me, we all learn in this lifetime. The big things and strongest habits start from very small, consistent and disciplined steps. There is only one person who should believe in you more than anyone else in your life: it is you!

Some targets and goals need to have proper planning and persistent actions, while some need to have more serendipity and inner trust. Overthinking "how my wish should come true" can create unnecessary energetic tensions. In the Universe of full potentiality, the desired outcome can happen in a very unexpected way. Our logical mind would not be able to assess and predict those circumstances.

I recommend you read some of the books mentioned in the next section. If you would like to increase the chances and bring additional energy and commitment to achieve your goal and make your wish come true, I would recommend utilizing some principles of asceticism (I can't name an author of this technique. However, it helped many people! I used this technique, too!) This is how you can do it:

1. Set intention – I am doing asceticism to receive "my Christmas (your wish here/target) present this year".
2. For this, I am voluntarily agreeing not to eat any sweets for the next 29 days, or not to eat any bread for the next 29 days, or I am committing to do 10 minutes of physical exercise every morning or every day; I will not do social media for three weeks.
3. This promise should be something where you do extra efforts to make it every day for the whole time, as you promised.
4. It is very important not to break this promise! Therefore, if your self-discipline is low, please do not do it. Otherwise, your intention or promise cannot be taken seriously; thus, your wish may not be taken seriously.
5. In order to release feel-good hormones (dopamine), please make a calendar for each day during the asceticism and each day mark it as "done" (using a green colour, for instance or your favourite colour) once you do the asceticism promise. It helps greatly to keep going! Tell yourself each time: "Well done! I can! Thank you."

If you broke the asceticism promise because of a valid reason, you must start all over again. The best is if you could do it the first time and finish with high commitment and self-discipline.

I personally wish you good luck and success with your endeavours.

Life is beautiful!

With love,
Kateryna Markhanova

Merry Christmas

and

Happy New year!

Recommended Books

Marie Kondo "Magic Cleaning"

Deepak Chopra "The Seven Spiritual Laws of Success"

Eckhart Tolle "The Power of Now: A Guide to Spiritual Enlightenment"

Joe Vitale "The Missing Secret: How to Use the Law of Attraction to Easily Attract What You Want...Every Time"

Acknowledgement

I am deeply thankful to family, my parents and my ancestors for life and all my gifts.

I am thankful to have learned from thought leaders such as Tony and Sage Robbins, Deepak Chopra, Eckhart Tolle, Colette Baron-Reid, my NLP teachers Richard Bandler and Alunika Dobrovolski, my RTT® hypnotherapy teacher Marisa Peer, spiritual teacher Natalia Tikhomirova, personal development and business coach Dmitry Karpachev, Simon Sinek, Joe Dispenza and many more of my personal mentors, teachers, and coaches.

My deep thank goes to Erik Seversen for guidance and help to publish this book, and my friend Amanda for her support in my writing endeavours.

And I am deeply thankful for each and every one of you who bought this book and applied this methodology!

About Author

Kateryna Markhanova was born in Ukraine, which was part of the USSR at the time. After successful graduation (MSc with honors) from one of the leading universities in Kiev, she worked on implementing the ISO Management Standards into the business processes of a large construction corporation. She had a dream of getting an international degree without having a financial budget for such kind of education abroad. Her dream came true as she won a scholarship for a one-year studyin Switzerland. Her journey had started to make one wish after another came true. Kateryna successfully completed the MSc Human-Environment Systems, ETH Zurich. Her professional background includes engineering, IT, financial services in a corporate environment, and coaching professionals with different backgrounds across the globe to achieve their life goals, feel joy and gain success. Since 2012, Kateryna has been studying psychology, spirituality, karmic numerology, high performance mindset, business and private relationships, manifestation principles, esoteric, principles of magic, and a variety of coaching methods and highly effective hypnotherapy techniques.

Some of her recent qualifications:

- Master Practitioner of Neuro-Linguistic Programming, NLP Life Trainings, Dr, Richard Bandler, 2019
- "Leadership Coaching Strategies," Harvard Professional Development Program, 2023
- Rapid Transformational Therapy®, Hypnotherapist, 2024

Kateryna Markhanova is the founder of IM Life Joy Success www.imlifejoysuccess.com. She lives in Switzerland, likes traveling and supports professionals to get happier and more fulfilled in their lives.

Dear Reader,

Being an independent author with a small marketing budget, reviews are very valuable and important for me.

If you enjoyed this book, I'd appreciate it if you could leave your sincere feedback. I read every single review because I love the feedback from my readers!

Thank you for buying this book!